Embracing the Day

Church Times Study Guide

Embracing the Day

Exploring Daily Prayer

Stephen Burns

CANTERBURY
PRESS
Norwich

© Stephen Burns 2006

First published in 2006 by the Canterbury Press Norwich
(a publishing imprint of Hymns Ancient & Modern Limited,
a registered charity)
9–17 St Alban's Place, London N1 0NX

www.scm-canterburypress.co.uk

Scripture quotations are from the New Revised Standard Version of
the Bible, copyright © 1989 by the Division of Christian Education of
the National Council of the Churches of Christ in the USA. Used by
permission. All rights reserved.

British Library Cataloguing in Publication data

A catalogue record for this book is available
from the British Library

ISBN 1-85311-710 2/978-1-85311-710-7

Typeset by Regent Typesetting, London
Printed and bound by
Gallpen Colour Print, Norwich

Contents

Introduction

Christian worship is patterned by cycles of time that embrace the day, the week, the year with its seasons, and, indeed, the human life-cycle, with its movement from womb to tomb, from cradle to grave. In this booklet, we shall explore developments in Christian daily prayer over time, with special attention to their legacy for the present. We consider:

- patterns of daily prayer, ancient and modern;
- aspects of daily prayer – praise, intercession, scripture; and
- a brief survey of some recent resources for daily prayer in the British churches.

Finally, we suggest a way to 'put the pieces together' and to establish a pattern for daily prayer.

Renewed interest in daily prayer

One of the remarkable developments of liturgical renewal in recent years has been the explosion of interest across the churches in daily prayer. For instance, for the very first time in worship books in their traditions, the new *Methodist Worship Book* (1999) and *Worship from the United Reformed Church* (2003–) have included orders for celebration of daily prayer by individuals or by small groups. And as we shall see, provisions in the Church of England have expanded in an extraordinary fashion so that, by comparison to a few pages in the *Alternative Service Book* (1980), a whole volume (over 900 pages) of *Common Worship* (2005) is now devoted to daily prayer.

Perhaps many factors have contributed to this new interest, and it might be that members of your study group relate personally to some of these possible reasons.

First, evangelical commentators have noted the recent sharp decline in practice of one of the mainstays of spiritual practice in the evangelical tradition, the 'quiet time'. Quiet time is a kind of shorthand used by evangelicals to refer to unstructured prayer wrapped around Bible reading, perhaps supported by some kind of commentary or notes such as those published by Scripture Union, Bible Reading Fellowship and other organizations. This practice of giving time daily to devotional scripture reading and personal prayer is perhaps less defining of recent evangelical spirituality than it once was, as it has come increasingly to be considered 'tired and outdated' (back cover, Alister McGrath, *Beyond the Quiet Time*) by many younger evangelical Christians. Influential writers within the evangelical tradition, such as Alister McGrath in his book *Beyond the Quiet Time*, have sought to rejuvenate this devotional practice, whilst at the same time commending characteristic styles of Bible reading in other Christian traditions – such as the Ignatian stress on imaginative 'indwelling' of biblical texts – which evangelicals generally have been absorbing eclectically into their spiritual practice in recent years. As part of this eclecticism, evangelicals have at the same time recently been expressing fresh interest in liturgical forms of prayer, as witnessed by the inclusion for a decade or more now of widely used liturgical texts in the likes of Spring Harvest materials. Changing patterns of evangelical spirituality have therefore opened up new possibilities for daily prayer as the churches have also sought to engage the evangelical constituency in their liturgical developments. We see in the experience of evangelical Christians a hopeful trend among many Christians, of all kinds, to be less defined by practices and habits particular or distinctive to their own inherited tradition, but more open to other styles and diverse expressions of Christian faith.

Second, in Britain, as further abroad, the Iona Community has published popular and attractive versions of daily prayer which have proved to be immensely popular and of great ecumenical significance. These are characteristically more informal, with more concrete kinds of images than those which were found in, for example, the *Alternative*

Service Book of the Church of England, and they invited a wide range of people into the practice of daily prayer whom the official resources had left untouched. Something of the flavour of the Iona liturgies can be gleaned from a sample such as

> O God of life, eternity cannot hold you,
> nor can our little words catch the magnificence of your kindness,
> yet in the small space of our hearts, and in silence,
> you can come close and repair us. . .
> (A Celtic Morning Liturgy, *A Wee Worship Book*, p. 17) © WGRG, 1989.
> Reproduced by permission

This kind of fresh, distinctive, pictorial language has introduced Christians across the traditions to set forms of prayer that may have in turn helped to introduce people to the sometimes more formal resources produced by the denominations. It should be noted, however, that the general trend of the denominational resources is towards greater informality (see below).

Furthermore, the daily prayer resources of the Franciscan tradition have been another highly significant feature of the changing landscape of liturgical prayer: *Celebrating Common Prayer*, based on the Franciscan office book, was published unofficially – though with great affirmation from many Anglican liturgical leaders – in 1992, and quickly came into very wide use across the Church of England, and before long in other denominations also. Anglicans of different church styles tended to respond extremely positively to *Celebrating Common Prayer* because, it seems, all were tired of the paucity of resources offered in the *Alternative Service Book* (again the contrast here was between a few pages of fixed text in the *ASB* and a wealth of materials across a whole book in *CCP*). *Celebrating Common Prayer* is in fact the basis for the new *Common Worship: Daily Prayer* and has shaped a new generation of liturgies for daily prayer both internationally and ecumenically.

One of the key features of *Celebrating Common Prayer* was its inclusion of simple forms for midday prayer and night prayer, and coupled with a resurgence of interest in retreats – with at least some of those who started to undertake retreats doing so in monastic settings – this has helped to re-engage the potential of 'the hours' downplayed at the Reformation, when most of the Protestant traditions preserved forms of prayer only for morning and evening-time. Monastic prayer developed into a sevenfold office ever twenty-four hours – Lauds, Prime, Terce, Sext, None, Vespers and Compline – and as retreatands have encountered these in monasteries they have seen the potential for at least some of these to be revived in parishes and for use at home. The inclusion in many newer prayerbooks of patterns of prayer for midday and night-time arise out of this appreciative encounter with monastic prayer.

Also, perhaps in part because the last pope, John Paul II, in a relatively short time-span canonized a plethora of new saints, many traditions have rediscovered and enriched their own *sanctorales* (calendars of remembrance of the saints). Focusing on the saints has been another way in which foci for daily prayer has developed in recent years. A wealth of official and semi-official resources has been produced for celebrating the saints in daily devotions, such as *Exciting Holiness* and *Celebrating the Saints*, companion volumes widely used across the Church of England.

Finally, both informal and official forms of daily prayer have been posted on the internet, and are updated day by day (for instance, at the Church of England's own website). It is yet to be seen how durable this way of praying proves to be, but for the time being such provisions are attractive to some people. If you do not have copies of *Common Worship: Daily Prayer* to hand, why not look up the Church of England's resources for daily prayer at www.cofe.anglican.org/worship/dailyprayer

Exercise

Quiet time, the Iona Community, the Franciscan tradition, retreats, the saints, and the internet make quite a diverse list of reasons for renewed interest in daily prayer! Do members of your group recognize in their own lives any of these factors shaping an interest in daily prayer?

Having considered some of the impulses behind the recent renewal of daily prayer in the churches, we next explore its origins in scripture and some developments in the history of the church.

1

Patterns of Daily Prayer

The development of early patterns of daily prayer

The idea of the day as a gift is deeply rooted in the scriptures. At the opening of Genesis, we read that 'there was evening and there was morning, the first day' (Genesis 1.5). From various other points in scripture, we can gain fragmentary sense of how the people of God were remembered as responding to the gift of a day: Exodus 29.38–39 relates the practice at the temple of offering two year-old lambs each day in sacrifice: one in the morning and the other in evening-time. Psalms and other Hebrew scriptures suggest how various individuals might have prayed through the day: Psalm 55.17 portrays the psalmist's 'complaints' being heard by God as they are uttered evening, morning and noon-time. Psalm 119.62 portrays the psalmist rising from sleep to pray at midnight. Psalm 141.2 suggests the psalmist's practice of prayer in the evening. Daniel 6.10 speaks of Daniel's habit of prayer three times a day, and Psalm 119.164 speaks about the offering of praise seven times a day.

Placing a number of New Testament texts adjacent to one another may also suggest early Christian practice of prayer at nine in the morning (Acts. 2.15), noon (Acts 10.9), three in the afternoon (Acts 3.1) and midnight (Acts 16.25).

What certainly *cannot* be deduced from these scriptural clues is any definite sense that these hours of prayer were kept formally by large numbers of people. However, taken together, they have left a strong legacy in the Christian tradition as forms of the 'liturgy of the hours' have sought to reflect the biblical witness to the faithful engaged in prayer through the day, as if 'without ceasing' (1 Thessalonians 5.17).

In the writings of the early Church, we find other clues that build upon the biblical legacy. In fact, the cluster of biblical texts that we have just outlined tend to recur in the writings of many early theologians on prayer. *The Didache*, or 'The Teaching of the Twelve Apostles' – a document that has also left its enduring mark on the practice of baptism and eucharist – suggests that the prayer Jesus taught, 'the Lord's prayer', is to be prayed three times a day. *The Didache* dates from the late first or second century AD. Writing around the beginning of the third century, Tertullian cites the authority of Daniel's practice of prayer three times a day to teach that a minimum of three prayer-times ought to be observed by his readers (*On Prayer*, 25–27). Tertullian's suggestion that prayer take place at the third, sixth and ninth hour (*On Fasting*, 10) also corresponds with contemporaneous writings of Clement of Alexandria, who writes to urge his readers on to 'perfection', praying throughout the whole of life rather than simply at the three times that were practised perhaps by many.

It seems that it did not take long before the three times of prayer common in at least some places at the turn of the third century had developed into a sevenfold pattern. *The Apostolic Tradition*, once ascribed to Hippolytus (and the source of the earliest known full text of eucharistic prayer) suggests a sevenfold pattern of daily prayer: on rising from sleep, and again at the third, sixth and ninth hours, then before the body rests, and midnight; finally, prayer should accompany cockcrow. 'Do not be lazy about praying', *The Apostolic Tradition* advises its readers! The same document also encourages people to *gather together* for at least some of these times of prayer, for the church is 'the place where the Holy Spirit flourishes'. According to *The Apostolic Tradition*, morning prayer, before work, is particularly suitable as a time of gathering with others, and furthermore, according to the document, is also a suitable time to allow for 'instruction in the word of God'.

We do not know any details about what comprised these times of prayer – what these early Christians said or did in their times of prayer – other than that, in *The Didache*, the prayer Jesus taught is seemingly of central importance. For many, perhaps these prayer times involved extempore prayer. And we may have a hint of the beginnings of the importance of the Psalms to later forms of Christian daily prayer in Tertullian's suggestion (at the beginning of the third century) that the 'pious' used Psalms ending in *alleluia* in their prayers.

Two ways of praying: 'city' and 'desert'

From the fourth century onwards, we do, however, begin to know more about the contents of daily prayer in various places. What we begin to see in this period is the emergence of different emphases, whose legacy is so strong it is now common to distinguish two types of daily prayer – one 'city', the other 'desert' – based on what we know of this period. The distinctions between daily prayer in the 'city' and daily prayer in the 'desert' have been of great importance in the compilation of contemporary forms of daily prayer, not least the Church of England's *Common Worship*, and so it is worthwhile exploring what these terms refer to.

It needs to be said that both 'city' and 'desert' are kinds of shorthand, and that they are used interchangeably by scholars with some other terms. 'City' prayer is also called 'urban' or 'cathedral' prayer; 'desert' prayer is also called 'monastic' prayer. Further, what is most important about them is not the *place* in which they occurred – city, desert, cathedral, wherever – but rather the different kinds of *style* of prayer they expressed and the different kinds of thinking that went into their *rationale*. Here, then, are some of the main distinguishing factors.

City prayer developed as prayer for assemblies: it was corporate, communal, congregational. That is not to say that it always gathered large crowds of people to it, but the thinking behind it was very much concerned with the Church. At the heart of city prayer is the remarkable, enduring and challenging sense that liturgical prayer is always expressed as part of the communion of saints, as George Guiver puts it: 'offered by all, in the indivisible oneness of Christ's body' (Guiver, *Company of Voices*, p. 83), and that its purpose is crucial to nothing less than the flourishing of the earth: this prayer is offered on behalf of all creation and has as its focus intercession for the world's salvation. Even if only two or three persons gather together for prayer, the sense in city prayer is very much of joining in something much greater and grand, echoing the prayer of heaven, mattering for the earth. Given the sense of purpose which developed around this style of prayer, it is not surprising that ceremonial practices came to lend it a kind of gravitas: it came to be led by ordained ministers, gathering others around them for prayer, music came to be important in this kind of prayer, and physical gestures and postures such as standing, kneeling and so on for different parts of the service came to be seen as integral to it. One of the most defining marks of city prayer is that the lighting of lamps came to be an important feature, accompanying opening song about Christ as the light of the world, and incense burned accompanying the recitation of Psalm 141: 'Let my prayer rise as incense before you'.

Desert prayer developed quite differently and had different ideas at its heart. By contrast to the emphasis on the communal in the city tradition, desert prayer developed much more as an individual activity. The word 'desert' suggests its solitary character; it reflects the stress in many monastic traditions on the 'cell' or enclosure. It simply did not require the company of others. And whereas city prayer had a definite outward focus to it – the needs of the world, the whole creation, the company of heaven – desert prayer, by contrast, had a much more inward orientation. It was essentially about nourishing the heart by means of meditation on scripture, particularly the Psalms. Unlike the city tradition, which used a select number of Psalms – sometimes to accompany ritual, such as Psalm 141 with the burning of incense – desert prayer stressed the value of spiritual reflection on all 150 Psalms, read in an ordered and disciplined way. In general there is much wider use of scripture in the desert tradition of prayer than in the city tradition. Furthermore, the inward orientation of the desert pattern meant that the ritual practices, such as lamp-lighting, that became key features of city prayer, did not develop in the desert style of prayer, and whereas city prayer tended to be led by the ordained ministers, as an expression of the congregation belonging to the wider church, desert prayer – where it took place in company, such as monastic communities – seems to have developed with less structured distinction between leaders and led; that is, people took turns to lead others in reading scripture, in prayer, and so on.

These, then, are some of the key differences between the two ways of praying that developed from the fourth century onwards, and they represent quite different trajectories of daily prayer, with different emphases, different ethos and different ideas behind them: one about witness to and prayer for the world, where the visibility of what is taking place is important as a reminder of God's presence, the other about the transformation of the heart by reflecting on God's word.

Exercise

Talk about which of the traditions of daily prayer, and which of their various emphases, most appeal to you.

As we shall see, many of the churches' contemporary resources for daily prayer, as other forms of daily prayer developed throughout the Church's history, have tried to allow for both city and desert tradition, with their different emphases, to be expressed, and to a certain extent to reconcile or 'blend' them. At different times, however, the emphases of one pattern have been stressed much more strongly than those of the other, as can be seen clearly in the developments of orders for daily prayer in the emerging Church of England of the sixteenth century.

The English Reformation

Martin Luther's experience as a monk falling behind in his duties to pray the 'daily offices', which seems to be central to his breaking from the Catholic Church, resounded strongly among Reformed believers: Luther wrote in his *Table Talk* of his time as a monk being marked by being too busy to devote enough time to keeping up with his obligation to recite the set forms of prayer for certain hours. Eventually he would need to spend a whole day doing nothing but reading his prayers so as to catch up. As he memorably put it, this made his 'head split'. A sense of the burden of the obligation to keep many daily offices of prayer came to be shared by many churches of the Reformation, among whom in fact only the Church of England maintained an obligation on its clergy to keep daily hours of prayer. Others tended to shy away from the imposition of this 'obligation' for fear of fuelling any sense that it might represent justification by works, as opposed to the central Reformation stress on being put right with God only by grace through faith. Still, what went on the English Church was by no means a reinstatement of the situation Luther loathed. The 1549 *Book of Common Prayer* cut the times of daily prayer down to two – morning and evening – and clearly stated that the purpose of its order was the 'great advancement of godliness', in which almost the whole of scripture would be read systematically through the course of a year (in fact, the New Testament, with the exception of Revelation, was read three times each year, and the complete psalter each month). In this, the 'desert' tradition was prioritized, although the 1549 book suggests that its reasons are soundly based on the 'ancient fathers', or early authorities. Stirring the clergy to godliness was important if the clergy were in their turn to 'exhort others by wholesome doctrine' and enable their people to become 'inflamed with the love of . . . true religion'.

It is true to say that over time in many places the practice of daily prayer was abandoned altogether, despite the efforts, at different times, of both evangelicals and Tractarians to revive it. And where it did survive, many parishes in the Church of England came to integrate aspects of the 'city' style of prayer into what was essentially a 'monastic' legacy from the *Book of Common Prayer*. That is, although the form of prayer did not evolve much from the definitive 1662 *Book of Common Prayer*, the understanding Anglican clergy brought to their daily prayer came to be more expansive than only the desert tradition. Throughout most of the twentieth century, even, most of the actual texts for daily prayer remained much the same as they had been in the early days of the English Reformation. It was not until the 1990s, when *Celebrating Common Prayer* emerged, that the revolution in the Church of England's resources for daily prayer began, and it might well be that the present time offers opportunity like no other for the church to rediscover the riches of daily prayer.

Exercise

How is daily prayer celebrated in your church? Do you know? Is there a gathering? Who goes along? Do you?

2

Aspects of Daily Prayer

The heart of all discipleship in the world is learning again and again
to pray.
(Don Saliers, *The Soul in Paraphrase*, p. 75)

We have now considered some of the history behind the current resources
for daily prayer, and we shall soon turn to look at those resources in more
detail. In the meantime, however, we pause, as it were, in this chapter to
consider some of the key theological aspects of daily prayer. With the help
of some modern theologians, some of the questions we shall consider are:
What is praise? What are we doing in intercession? Why bother to read
the Psalms? Without a grasp of the importance of these questions, the
renewal of daily prayer is unlikely to be durable or transforming.

Praise

Praise, write Daniel Hardy and David Ford, is 'an attempt to cope with
the abundance of God's love' (*Jubilate: Theology in Praise*, p. 6). It is at the
centre of the celebration of the Eucharist: 'it is indeed right, it is our duty
and our joy, at all time and in all places, to give you thanks and praise'
(*Common Worship*, eucharistic prayer A), and daily prayer amplifies that
praise, providing other times and places for its expression, a daily 'attempt
to cope' with the abundance of God.

Reflecting on the 'strange logic' of praise, Hardy and Ford suggest that
it is a kind of 'perfecting perfection' in that it is 'an enhancement of what
is already valued' which is marked by free and generous response:

When we find something of quality and express our appreciation, that very expression adds something to the situation. This is even more so in the case of praise of a person. To recognise worth and to respond to it with praise is to create a new relationship. This new mutual delight is itself something of worth, an enhancement of what is already valued.

There need be no end to this: there can be an infinite spiral of free response and expression of it in look or word or act. Like lovers writing letters or just looking into each other's eyes, the expression of appreciation is not an optional extra in the relationship; it is intrinsic to its quality, and is also a measure of all behaviour within it. (*Jubilate*, p. 6)

Exercise

How would you explain the meaning of praise?

David Ford elaborates on these ideas when he writes with another colleague of the possibility of 'praising open' the future: 'Praise opens up the horizon within which present conditions can be seen to contradict the life and will of God; it energizes commitment to a new and different future; and it helps set an agenda for change' (David Ford and Alistair McFadyen, 'Praise', in Peter H. Sedgwick, ed., *God in the City: Essays and Reflections for the Archbishop of Canterbury's Urban Theology Group* (London: Mowbray, 1995), 95–104, p. 98). This dimension of praise is important, for without its stretching towards future transformation, it could perhaps collapse into a kind of evasion of intolerable aspects of present experience. Participation in praise, then, ought to be a life-changing experience, powerful enough to shake up change and lead to fuller life.

And thanks goes hand-in-hand with praise. Hardy and Ford speak of praise's close companion as 'completing what is completed': 'When something has happened that is good then thanks is one way (and perhaps the most fully personal way) for that to overflow into the present and the future' (*Jubilate*, p. 7). An ancient eucharistic prayer, that known as Addai and Mari, suggests what the human person engaged in thanks and praise might look like: it suggests that the eucharistic prayer is prayed with 'open mouths and uncovered faces' (R. C. D. Jasper and G. J. Cuming, eds, *Prayers of the Eucharist: Early and Reformed*, p. 43) as if astonished and amazed by the grace being celebrated!

If we are to celebrate daily prayer in the 'city' tradition – or, indeed, if we are to celebrate the Eucharist – we need to appreciate the power of praise. In the contemporary resources for daily prayer, the keynote of praise is struck in the words of Psalm 70.1 which open morning prayer:

O Lord, open our lips
and our mouth shall proclaim your praise.

But it is perhaps present especially in the great prayers of blessing which follow closely on from those opening words. Here is part of the 'thanksgiving for the word' from *Common Worship*:

Blessed are you, Lord our God.
How sweet are your words to the taste,
sweeter than honey to the mouth.
How precious are your commands for our life,
more than the finest gold in our hands.
How marvellous is your will for the world,
unending is your love for the nations.
Our voices shall sing of your promises
and our lips declare your praise . . .
(*Common Worship Services and Prayers for the Church of England*, p. 46)
© The Archbishops' Council 2000. Reproduced by permission.

Blessing light

This beautiful prayer falls at the opening of some orders for daily prayer in *Common Worship*. Another key feature of the opening parts of orders for daily prayer is the focus on the symbol and imagery of light, accompanied by praise of Christ as 'light of the world', one of John's Gospel's 'I am' statements made by the saviour. Many new orders for daily prayer have revived an ancient Christian custom of ceremonial lamp-lighting at the start of the liturgy, perhaps accompanied by a prayer (and/or scripture reading) which accentuates the motif of light, as in this example from the Episcopal Church of the USA:

> Almighty God, we give you thanks for surrounding us, as daylight fades, with the brightness of the vesper light; and we implore you of your great mercy that, as you enfold us with the radiance of this light, so you would shine into our hearts the brightness of your Holy Spirit; through Jesus Christ our Lord. *Amen.* (*The Book of Common Prayer* [1979], Episcopal Church of the United States of America)

This ceremony is a powerful beginning to prayer in the evening, and certainly has deep roots in the Christian tradition, and its popularity suggests that it has caught the imagination of the contemporary church. That is not to say, however, that it is unproblematic, for use of light and darkness imagery all too easily slides into the danger that 'racism is perpetuated when the colour black is used in negative, and white in positive, ways' as Mukti Barton contends. Part of her argument is that in some languages – including her own Bengali – blackness and darkness are quite distinct, although in English, the overlappings of the two terms are much more ambiguous, at times synonymous. Consequently, European interpretations of the Bible (itself 'from the East') and its imagery may muddle originally biblical and purely European meanings, leading to both confusion and harm (Mukti Barton, 'I am Black and Beautiful', *Black Theology: An International Journal* 2.2 (2004), 167–87, p. 167). Great care is, then, needed about this ceremony – and of course other dimensions of Christian worship, like the liturgical seasons (in which Advent also plays on the light and darkness theme) if it is to be helpful for all God's people.

Alongside the blessing of light, another symbol has also been reintroduced into the practice of daily prayer in at least some places, and that is the burning of incense. This vivid image of prayer rising as though before God's face, carrying the prayers of the saints (see Revelation 8.4) is often accompanied – as in ancient orders for daily prayer – by recitation of Psalm 141.

Lamp-lighting and use of incense are just two notable examples of the ways in which contemporary orders for daily prayer sometimes place great stress on the ways in which symbols can serve to set a helpful ambience for prayer. *Worship from the United Reformed Church* suggests candles and an open Bible as good visual foci during daily prayer; *The Methodist Worship Book* affirms the use of 'objects such as crosses or candles' (p. 1) and *Common Worship: Daily Prayer* for the Church of England recommends careful attention to space and symbolism in celebration, and in fact makes extensive suggestions about this dimension of the liturgy. It is recommended that a small group be seated 'in a semi-circle' (p. x), perhaps with a lectern holding an open Bible as a visual focus. Being seated around the font is an alternative suggestion (also p. x). Use of other Christian symbols – 'a cross, a candle, an icon, a symbol of the season . . .' such as, in Lent, a rough wooden cross (p. xi) – are all suggested, as are 'the lighting of candles' and 'the burning of incense' (p. xi). Individuals and groups engaged in daily prayer will no doubt act in different ways on these encouragements, but the stress on the symbolic aspects of the liturgy found in so many denominational resources is at least an invitation to think of worship 'beyond the words'.

Exercise

How important to you are the 'externals' of worship?

Intercession

When we intercede, we 'look in the direction where God's love is looking', writes Don Saliers (*The Soul in Paraphrase*, p. 80). Intercession is a sharing in the compassion of God towards the world God loves, and to its peoples. As the word 'compassion' suggests, this prayer involves a 'suffering with' (com-passion) others. Intercession is, therefore, a kind of imagining oneself into the 'shoes', the experience, of another so that 'feeling of concern leads to responsible action' (Taylor, *The Go-Between God*, p. 242). At the heart of Christian prayer, the prayer that Jesus taught includes intercession for the reign of God to come on earth, for provision of the basic needs of human beings ('daily bread'), and for the kinds of exchanges in human affairs which support human flourishing ('forgive us our sins, as we forgive . . .'). Perhaps above all, though, the prayer Jesus taught asserts that God is 'our Father' and not simply concerned with 'my' care. To pray to 'our Father' demands not a sentimental view of God, but solidarity with others. To learn to pray this prayer is *inevitably* to see oneself as related to others, including those in extremity.

The idea of intercession as a share in God's compassion has endured as a strong motivator to Christians to intercede, and it stretches Christians' concerns not only beyond the self but well beyond their significant others and immediate circles. 1 Timothy 2.1–4 is a scriptural injunction to pray for 'kings and all who are in high positions', but the heart of the challenge of intercession is undoubtedly Christ's own call to pray for one's enemies.

Exercise

For whom do you pray?

The forms in *Common Worship: Daily Prayer* suggest many different expressions of intercession, from simple extempore prayer, to different kinds of forms (pages 366–99). The little-used Litany (pages 400–4) is important as a challenging reminder of the breadth of concern that intercession might express. The 'cycle of intercession' (pages 362–5), which suggests foci for intercession on different days of the week, and which is incorporated into services where extempore prayer is invited, is an encouragement to keep daily prayer outward-looking and broad in its concerns. For instance, intercession on Wednesday might focus on the social services, all who work in the criminal justice system, victims and perpetrators of crime, the work of aid agencies throughout the world and those living in poverty or under oppression.

The Psalms

In the 'desert' tradition of daily prayer, and again in the emphasis adopted by the emergent Church of England, the Psalms were a mainstay of daily prayer. In fact, the Psalms have remained a major and durable feature of most patterns of daily prayer across the Christian traditions, and they are central also to the contemporary resources. Popular, fresh translations of the Psalms – perhaps most notably Eugene Peterson's *The Message* version, in which, for instance, we read at the opening of Psalm 27 'Light, space, zest! That's God!' – have helped to open up the Psalms to a new generation of readers.

The Psalms have remained so engaging for Christians (and of course Jews) over time because they not only teach a language for praising God, but also embrace lament, despair and anger as well as the deepest joy. Don Saliers points out the 'full emotional range' of the Psalms that engage the wide breadth of human experience, or what Saliers calls in another place 'humanity at full stretch' (*Worship and Spirituality*, p. 1). By touching on all of life, the Psalms resist limiting the sense of divine presence, of narrowing God's concern for the human condition or God's involvement in human affairs to joyous feeling. Indeed, the Psalms may 'take us places we do not wish to go' as well as into 'luminous expanses of doxology' (Don Saliers, 'David's Song in Our Land', in Blair Gilmer Meeks, ed., *The Landscape of Praise: Readings in Liturgical Renewal*, p. 240), and by so doing teach the reference of all things to God.

Exercise

What sense do you make of the Psalms?

Moreover, for Christians, it is the capacity of the Psalms to embrace joy and sorrow that offers a particular way of relating to Jesus. For the Psalms, of course, were the song-book of Jesus, and what the Gospels suggest of his own use of the psalter underlines the demanding nature of its content, its potential to take its singers to places they may not wish to go. Indeed, it is in the horror of the cross where Jesus' own use of the Psalms is most intense: two of the seven recorded words from the cross are in fact direct citations: 'My God, my God, why have you forsaken me?' (Psalm 22.1); 'Into your hands I commit my spirit' (Psalm 31.5). Ultimately, for Christians, the promise of daily praying the Psalms is that Christ might be encountered in and through them, and Christ known in both joy and sorrow.

3

Looking at Some Recent Resources for Daily Prayer

This brief chapter surveys some of the main features of some new forms of daily prayer in a range of British churches. As noted in the Introduction, *Worship from the United Reformed Church* includes 'a new element' (foreword) – a form of 'daily worship' (pp. 97–102) intended for either individual or group-use. Its simple order is based around the structure of the Lord's Prayer, elaborating on each petition in turn. The *Methodist Worship Book* also includes for the first time in British Methodist history a considerable – and being first, significant – slice on 'daily prayer' (pp. 1–25). It is distinguished from 'morning, afternoon or evening services' (pp. 26–59) in that daily prayer is 'not intended for public worship on Sundays' but rather 'may be used for daily personal or corporate devotion' (p. 1). The Methodist book explicitly recognizes that daily prayer may also be used 'in conjuction with' other devotional material (perhaps 'quiet time' notes?). In both the United Reformed Church and the Methodist Church material, the forms include seasonal and daily variants and extensive use of permissive rubrics – 'if desired', 'selected freely', 'or some other' – although an interesting feature of the Methodist book is that many of the texts for prayer it suggests for use as a kind of 'default' text are quite consciously chosen from the very early centuries. Texts such as the *Benedictus, Te Deum, Venite, Jubilate, Magnificat* and *Nunc Dimittis*, all of which had a place in daily prayer in the wider western Christian tradition, are deliberately included.

As we also noted earlier, the contrast between the *Alternative Service Book* of 1980 and the Church of England's new forms of daily prayer is quite remarkable. The *ASB* order for morning and evening prayer consisted of an unaltered rigid set form for use every day amounting to no more than a few pages of texts. Its use was obligatory for clergy. By contrast, *Common Worship: Daily Prayer*, based on *Celebrating Common Prayer*, is, it emphasizes, conceived as a prayer book for the whole people of God (e.g. p. 76 speaks of the 'privilege and duty which belongs to all God's priestly people'), and runs to hundreds of pages, many of which are a 'directory' from which variable items may be selected. (On the dynamics of the 'directory' approach, see the highly important *New Patterns for Worship* (London: Church House Publishing, 2002), the 'teaching resource' in the *Common Worship* series.)

People praying with the Methodist or United Reformed Church resources will find it much easier to pick up their prayerbooks and use their orders of daily prayer. Making the most of the new Church of England provision is a little more complicated, but it does at least promise the kind of richness and variety that Anglicans praying with earlier set forms, such as the ASB, so widely seemed to tire of. Taking a closer look at the current Anglican rites may therefore promise refreshment to people in other traditions who may be new to using prayer-book patterns for daily prayer and whose denominational resources for daily prayer are not as expansive as *Common Worship*.

In fact, it is possible to construct from *Common Worship: Daily Prayer* a very wide range of forms of daily prayer, from the very simple to the highly elaborate. It is 'intended to help each person or group to make the most suitable and satisfying use' of it (p. viii), and has in mind not only individuals and small groups, but 'a parish at prayer' and 'religious communities' (i.e. monastic settings). 'There are many possible combinations' (p. ix) of how its wide resources can be employed.

It does, however, provide structures – albeit sometimes minimal ones. For instance, it recognizes that one form, 'prayer during the day,' will be used to do no more than 'provide a framework for a daily Quiet Time and Bible study' (p. 30), and simply frames scripture reading and extempore prayer with a couple of suggested scripture sentences. Variation, improvisation (p. 80), extemporization, 'personal and corporate Bible study' (p. 33) are all envisaged as being proper components of this celebration and 'silence, study, song' are repeatedly encouraged (e.g. pp. 36, 39, 41, etc.) as alternative and appropriate responses to the reading of scripture in all of the orders. This makes 'prayer during the day' one of the most informal of all the current resources both within and beyond the Church of England. This feature is probably the most significant contribution of *Common Worship: Daily Prayer*, recognizing the inadequacy of more formal forms of prayer if daily prayer is to be recovered as a practice embraced by the laity as well as a discipline imposed upon the clergy. At the same time, it is possible to use *Common Worship: Daily Prayer* to construct more dense and elaborate liturgical forms, resembling at least four of the traditional monastic offices, and the orders for morning, evening and night prayer, although also allowing considerable flexibility, are full offices of scripture readings, including a rich complement of scriptural and traditional canticles (that is, songs, drawn mainly from scripture).

In keeping with some of the emphases of the 'desert' tradition, *Common Worship: Daily Prayer* also makes much of the importance of the Psalms as a staple of daily prayer: 'at least one Psalm should be included on each occasion' (p. 32), and a number of ways of reading the psalms are outlined: in a single voice, antiphonally, responsorially, corporately, and using refrains either said or sung (p. xi). It is suggested that the content of each particular psalm itself should determine the form in which it is presented, with form serving the content. *Common Worship: Daily Prayer* also recommends 'singing, however simply' (p. x, p. 76) whenever possible, and in every aspect stresses the great importance of participation: 'it is good to involve a number of people in leading' (p. x, p. 77) the services.

What we find in these various resources is great encouragement to explore how daily prayer might work best for particular individuals and particular communities. There are also plenty of patterns to try out, ideas to employ and alternatives to test. By way of conclusion, then, we look at some basic questions to do with getting started on a pattern of daily prayer.

Conclusion

There is probably little future – and little attraction – about daily prayer surviving as a preserve of the clergy, quite possibly holed up alone in church buildings and using forms long lost on the laity. However, at a time when churches are recovering or discovering the 'shared ministry' of the 'priesthood of all believers' (or 'all believers' share in the priesthood of Christ'), there is surely great potential in the Church's new resources for daily prayer to nurture fresh energy for Christian discipleship.

Having explored something of the history of daily prayer, touched on the theological dimensions of some of its aspects, and explored in a little detail some contemporary materials for daily prayer, the challenge now comes to try them out!

The place to start is probably with the resources themselves. The last chapter mentions three books – one Anglican, one Methodist and one United Reformed Church – in which resources for daily prayer can be found. The Anglican materials at least can also be found on the internet at *http://www.cofe.anglican.org/worship/dailyprayer/* where there is a very helpful 'daily prayer feed' that compiles a simple structure and resources for prayer each day. The United Reformed Church and the Methodist Church unfortunately have not published web-based versions of their resources for daily prayer, although the Methodist Church does publish a 'Prayer of the Day' at *http://www.methodist.org.uk/index. cfm?fuseaction=pandw.potd* and this might be used in a simple pattern of daily prayer. (Similarly, the American United Methodists publish a daily devotion, which includes a scripture reading and simple prayer, on the web at *http://www.upperroom.org/devotional/default.asp*) Fuller versions of daily prayer are produced by the American Methodist Order of St Luke at *http://www.saint-luke.org/community.html#daily* All of these are worth exploring, as are many other good web-based resources for prayer which can be accessed through the Evangelical Lutheran Church in Canada's excellent worship website *http://www.worship.ca*

Others may wish to compile a very simple order of service to guide their own prayer. This is not complicated and may consist of:

- An opening sentence of scripture.
- A prayer of praise (perhaps a simple extempore prayer).
- A Psalm.
- A Bible reading.
- A time for response to the reading – perhaps time of stillness to reflect on the reading or, if with others, a brief discussion.
- Some prayer, with an accent on intercession.
- The prayer Jesus taught.
- A concluding prayer.

Psalm 70.1 is perhaps the most obvious verse of scripture to use at the opening; the 'thanksgiving for the word' cited above in Chapter 3 might be used as an alternative to extempore prayer for the opening prayer of praise, and daily Bible reading notes might be used in response to the Bible reading. Many helpful cycles of intercession which will help to keep prayer fresh are available from a range of different sources (such as *http://www. cofe.anglican.org/worship/liturgy/commonworship/texts/daily/prayers/ cycle.html*) and lively set forms of intercession can be found in abundance at *http://www.cofe.anglican.org/worship/liturgy/commonworship/texts/ newpatterns/texts/sectionf.html*

Those using daily Bible notes will find a structured pattern of habitual Bible reading; others will need to find one. A number of churches produce their own (for instance, the Church of England's daily lectionary, intended primarily for congregations gathering for communion, is on the web at *http://www.cofe.anglican.org/worship/liturgy/commonworship/texts/ lect/lectfront.html*, although perhaps a better place to begin is with the schematic readings around various themes at *http://www.cofe.anglican. org/worship/liturgy/commonworship/texts/newpatterns/texts/sectionc. html*).

It is then a case of putting these pieces together, remembering of course that attention to space and symbols is important as well as attention to words!

Compiling a simple order made up of these different bits and pieces is something that individuals might do themselves, or small groups can attempt together. There are many possibilities for how daily prayer may be undertaken by either individuals or groups. Apart from its obvious potential to help cultivate personal disciplines of intimacy with God, it may in fact be increasingly necessary for congregations to pour energy into nurturing some form of daily prayer among their dispersed members so as to nurture the biblical literacy necessary to make the symbols and stories of common worship meaningful.

References and Further Reading

Liturgical texts referred to in the text

Common Worship: Daily Prayer, 2005, London: Church House Publishing

The Methodist Worship Book, 1999, Peterborough: Methodist Publishing House

New Patterns for Worship, 2002, London: Church House Publishing

Worship from the United Reformed Church, 2003, London: United Reformed Church

Atwell, Robert, ed., 2004, *Celebrating the Saints: Daily Spiritual Readings*, Norwich: Canterbury Press

Brother Tristram, ed., 2003, *Exciting Holiness*, 2nd edn, Norwich: Canterbury Press

Iona Community, *A Wee Worship Book*, 3rd edn, 1989, Glasgow: Wild Goose Publications

Other references and further reading

Bradshaw, Paul, 1995, *Two Ways of Praying*, London: SPCK

Bradshaw, Paul and Jones, Simon, 2005, 'Daily Prayer', in Paul Bradshaw, ed., *A Companion to Common Worship*, London: SPCK, pp. 1–33

Earey, Mark, 2000, *Producing Your Own Orders of Service*, London: Church House Publishing

Fletcher, Jeremy and Myers, Gilly, 2002, *Using Common Worship: Daily Prayer*, London: Church House Publishing

Gillett, David, 1993, *Trust and Obey: Explorations in Evangelical Spirituality*, London: Darton, Longman & Todd

Guiver, George, 1988, *A Company of Voices: Daily Prayer and the People of God*, London: SPCK

Hardy, Daniel and Ford, David, 1984, *Jubilate: Theology in Praise*, London: Darton, Longman & Todd; recently republished as David Ford and Daniel Hardy, 2005, *Living in Praise*, London: Darton, Longman & Todd

Jasper, R. C. D. and Cuming, G. J., eds, 1987, *Prayers of the Eucharist: Early and Reformed*, 3rd edn, Collegeville, MN: Liturgical Press

Koinig, John, 1998, *Rediscovering New Testament Prayer: Boldness and Blessing in the Name of Jesus*, 2nd edn, Harrisburg, PA: Morehouse

McGrath, Alister, 1995, *Beyond the Quiet Time: Practical Evangelical Spirituality*, London: Triangle

Peterson, Eugene, 1994, *The Message: Psalms*, Colorado Springs, CO: NavPress

Saliers, Don, 1991, *The Soul in Paraphrase: Prayer and the Religious Affections*, 2nd edn, Akron, OH: Order of St Luke

Saliers, Don, 1994, *Worship as Theology*, Nashville, TN: Abingdon Press

Saliers, Don, 1996, *Worship and Spirituality*, 2nd edn, Akron, OH: Order of St Luke

Saliers, Don, 1997, 'David's Song in Our Land', in Blair Gilmer Meeks, ed., *The Landscape of Praise: Readings in Liturgical Renewal*, Valley Forge, PA: Trinity Press International, pp. 235–41

Stancliffe, David, 2003, *God's Pattern: Shaping Our Worship, Ministry and Life*, London: SPCK

Taylor, John, 1979, *The Go-Between God: The Holy Spirit and the Christian Mission*, Oxford: Oxford University Press

Vann, Jane Rogers, 2002, *Gathered Before God: Worship-Centered Church Renewal*, Louisville: Westminster John Knox Press

Woolfenden, Gregory, 2004, *Daily Liturgical Prayer: Origins and Theology*, Aldershot: Ashgate